D1055243

This delightful Fireside book is the latest in a series that have been specially imagined to help grown-ups learn about the world around them. Using large clear type, simple and easy-to-grasp words, frequent repetition, and thoughtful matching of text with pictures, these books should be a great comfort to grown-ups.

The Fireside Grown-up Guides understand that the world is just as confusing to a forty-year-old as it is to a four-year-old. By breaking down the complexity of grown-up life into easy-to-digest nuggets of information, and pairing them with colorful illustrations even a child could under-stand, the Fireside Grown-up Guides prove that being a grown-up can be as simple as "look and remember."

The publishers gratefully acknowledge assistance provided by Josh Weinstein, Egregius Professor of Reference at Mars University and Reader-in-Residence at Springfield Library, in compiling this book.

THE FIRESIDE GROWN-UP GUIDE TO

THE
HUSBAND

by J. A. HAZELEY, N.S.F.W.
and J. P. MORRIS, O.M.G.

Authors of *Eat Yourself Fat*

TOUCHSTONE
New York   London   Toronto   Sydney   New Delhi

This is a husband.

He may look complicated,
but he is in fact very simple.

He runs on sausages and beer.

The husband knows many things.

For example, he knows how many stairs there are, in case he arrives home unable to see them properly.

The husband likes to do simple repairs, like changing the washer on a faucet.

Afterward, he likes to talk at great length about what a struggle it was and will want to be treated as if he has invented a machine that turns farts into gold.

The husband has a very big memory. He can remember football scores, all his old car license plate numbers, and most of *Caddyshack*.

But he cannot remember what his wife asked him to bring back from the store. This is because his brain is full up, not because he was not listening.

On special occasions, the husband and wife dress up to go out together.

Emma has lots of outfits. Graham has one suit. It is called His Suit, and he has had it for a long time.

Graham likes His Suit, even though it has not fit in years, has a four-inch tear in the seat, and makes him look like a burglar in court.

The husband finds some things very difficult. Being wrong is one of these things.

When he is wrong, the husband will refer to the times he was right, even if they date back many years.

It is important for the husband to pretend that he had no life before he was married, especially if he was married before he was married.

Jimbo works hard all week
and has only a few hours on
the weekend to spend with his
family.

He spends these hours watching
sports.

The wife likes to read romantic fiction. The books are a fantasy and an escape for her.

The husband does not waste his time on silly stories. He likes to read books about things that really happened and tales of real men.

Reading these will be invaluable if he ever has to land on the moon or be a Navy SEAL or help manage the New England Patriots.

This is what the inside of Tim's head looks like.

It also contains pictures of some ladies before they have put their clothes on.

None of the ladies is Tim's wife.

The husband always has the right tool for the job.

A screwdriver in the kitchen for opening shrink-wrapped frozen pizzas.

A shoe on the sideboard for putting up pictures.

And a bread knife taped behind the toilet for dispatching monsters.

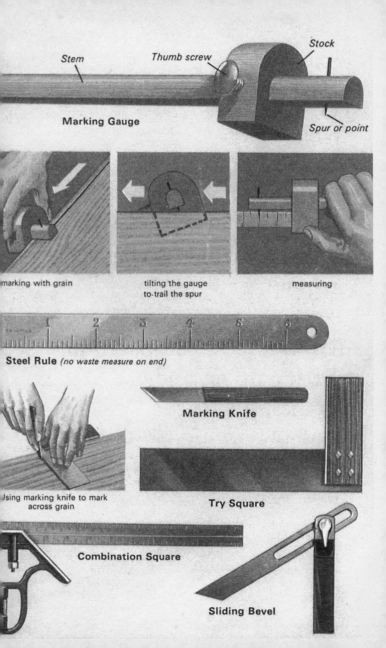

Marking Gauge

Stem

Thumb screw

Stock

Spur or point

marking with grain

tilting the gauge to trail the spur

measuring

Steel Rule *(no waste measure on end)*

Using marking knife to mark across grain

Marking Knife

Try Square

Combination Square

Sliding Bevel

The husband finds it difficult to express his feelings. At this men's talk therapy group, husbands are encouraged to open up.

Three of these husbands are playing poker, and one of them is reading a book about ghosts.

They are not talking.

In Japan, you can buy a robot husband.

This is M.1., a fully motorized electronic husband. He can move furniture, barbecue, clear gutters, carve roasts, install TVs, kick and catch balls, and is even programmed to apologize.

Sadly, scientists cannot work out how to stop him burping.

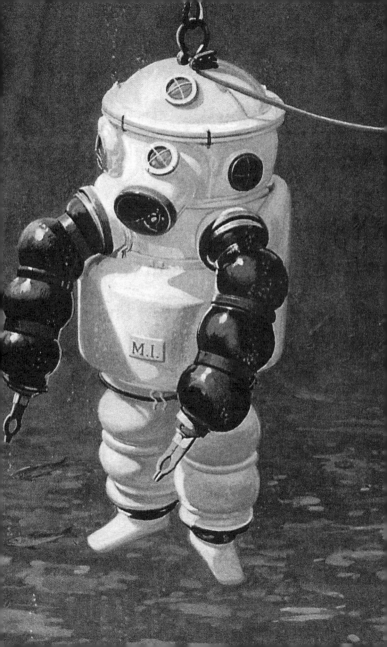

Glenn explains himself very badly.

This is so he can say he is misunderstood.

Husbands like to meet with friends for a chat.

This husband has been talking to his friends for five and a half hours about which Doctor Who would win in a game of hide-and-seek.

He has forgotten to ask whether his friends' wives and children are still living with them, or even alive.

As the husband grows older, he starts to make lots of funny little noises.

He sighs as he gets out of a chair, and talks like Inspector Clouseau when he feels conversation has dried up.

He also *pom-pom-poms* as he goes from room to room.

This is to remind himself that he's still here.

Nellie and Ross are now the parents of a baby boy. Ross was there for the birth. Nellie would have preferred him to be here, but he was there.

Nellie is delighted to be a mom and cannot stop looking at her newborn.

Ross is looking at the nurses.

Husbands like nurses.

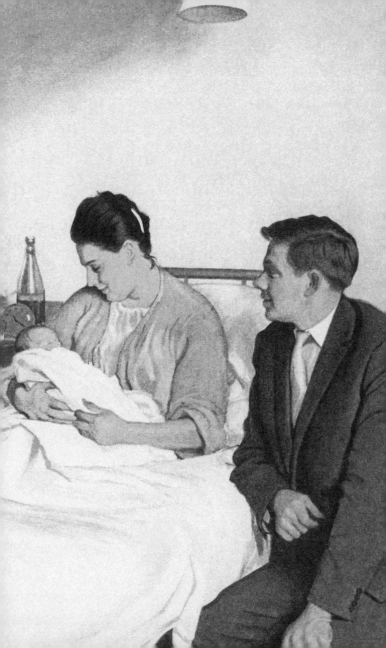

Helen complains that Stuart spends too much time on his computer and telephone.

"Let's have a family Sunday without them," says Helen. "Just you, me, and Sally."

Stuart has bought a newspaper that weighs more than Sally.

"Shh," says Stuart.

Nick is out for a picnic with his wife and children. The au pair has also come along.

Nick has to sit with one leg up to disguise the unfortunate way that the au pair brings out the beast in him.

Hugh moved to the country to give his family a better life.

His journey to work in the city now takes three hours each way.

He is only at home when his wife and children are asleep, which has given them all a better life.

Jim has just found all the clutch bags he has bought his wife as Christmas and birthday presents. She said she lost them but she has hidden them in the garage.

Jim and Rebecca have been husband and wife for thirty-one years and he still does not know what she likes.

This Christmas, he will probably get her another bag just the same.

Husbands like do-it-yourself.

Today, Richard has hung a door so it gets stuck on the hall carpet and assembled a flat-pack chest of drawers with three mysterious metal shapes left over—and he did it all by himself.

Now he is repeatedly driving up and down the same half-mile stretch of road and not asking for directions himself.

The husband hears as much as 30 percent of what is said to him.

Many husbands are traditional and do not believe in listening before marriage.

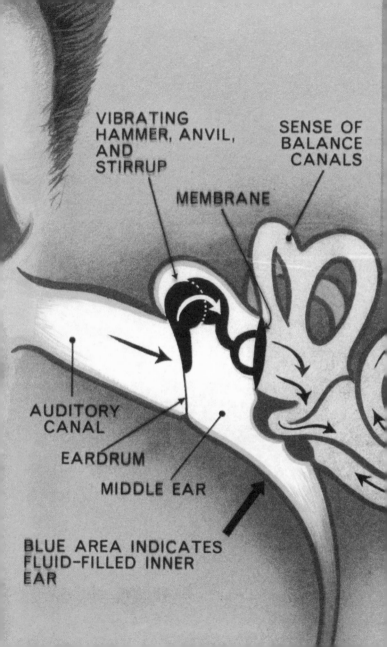

The husband likes things to be in order. At home, the DVDs, wrenches, shirts, golf clubs, wine, spare lightbulbs, and the kitchen knives are in an order that the husband understands.

Alan is putting his family's shoes in alphabetical order. This will make them harder to find, but at least it will be logical.

Alan's wife sometimes cries herself to sleep.

TOUCHSTONE
An Imprint of Simon & Schuster, Inc.
1230 Avenue of the Americas
New York, NY 10020

First Touchstone hardcover edition October 2016

TOUCHSTONE and colophon are registered trademarks of Simon & Schuster, Inc.

For information about special discounts for bulk purchases,
please contact Simon & Schuster Special Sales at 1-866-506-1949
or business@simonandschuster.com.

The Simon & Schuster Speakers Bureau can bring authors to your live event.
For more information or to book an event, contact the Simon & Schuster Speakers Bureau
at 1-866-248-3049 or visit our website at www.simonspeakers.com.

Manufactured in Mexico

1   3   5   7   9   10   8   6   4   2

Library of Congress Cataloging-in-Publication Data

Names: Hazeley, Jason, author. | Morris, Joel (Comedy writer), author.
Title: The Fireside grown-up guide to the husband / by J. A. Hazeley and J. P. Morris.
Other titles: Husband | Husband
Description: New York : Touchstone, 2016. | Series: The Fireside grown-up guides
Identifiers: LCCN 2016011235 | ISBN 9781501150739 (hardback)
Subjects: LCSH: Husbands—Humor. | Marriage—Humor. | BISAC: HUMOR / Form /
Parodies. | HUMOR / Topic / Marriage & Family. | HUMOR / Topic / Relationships.
Classification: LCC PN6231.H8 H39 2016 | DDC 306.872/2—dc23
LC record available at https://lccn.loc.gov/2016011235

ISBN 978-1-5011-5073-9
ISBN 978-1-5011-5074-6 (ebook)

THE ARTISTS

Martin Aitchison
Robert Ayton
John Berry
David Carey
R. Embleton
Roger Hall
Frank Hampson
Jack Matthew
Jorge Nuñez
Gerald Witcomb

THE FIRESIDE GROWN-UP GUIDES TO

MINDFULNESS

THE
HUSBAND

THE
MOM

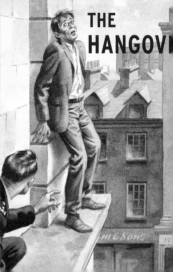

THE
HANGOVE